Piano • Vocal • Guitar

#1 SONGS OF THE 90'S

As listed on the Billboard Hot 100 Singles Chart

WITHDRAWN

ISBN 0-7935-1646-3

HL Hal Leonard Publishing Corporation

7777 West Bluemound Road P.O. Box 13819 Milwaukee, WI 53213

BABY BABY

Words and Music by AMY GRANT
and KEITH THOMAS

Stop for a min-ute. Ba - by, I'm so glad you're mine, _____ yeah. _

Stop for a min-ute. Ba - by, they're so glad you're mine, _

You're mine.

oh yeah. _____ And ev - er since the day you

put my heart in mo - tion, ba - by, I real - ize that there's

BECAUSE I LOVE YOU
(The Postman Song)

Words and Music by
WARREN ALLEN BROOKS

1. I got your let-ter from the post-
2.,3. If you should feel that

man just the oth-er day so I de-cid-ed to write you this song
I don't real-ly care and that you're start-ing to lose ground.

to be your light, ___ to be ___ your guide. ___

Repeat and Fade

BLACK CAT

Words and Music
JANET JACKSO

You're a reb - el now don't give a damn.__ Al - ways carry -
keep.__ Don't you tell your - self that it's o - kay.__ Sick and tir -

ing on with the gang.__ I'm tryin' to tell you boy. It's a mis - take.__
ed of all of your games.__ And you want me to stay ah, __ bet - ter change.__

You won't re - al - ize_____ 'til it's too late.__
Makes no sense to me,_____ your cra - zy ways.__

B7

A7

Don't un - der-stand why you in - sist on ways of liv - in' such a dan - ger - ous life.__

D.S. al Coda

Livin' on the edge.

CODA

Black cat, nine lives, short__ days, long__ nights. Liv - in' on the edge, not a -

fraid to die. Heart - beat real strong but__ not for __ long.

Bet - ter watch your step or you're gon - na die.

D(no3rd)   E(no3rd)

gon - na die.

BLACK VELVET

Moderately slow bluesy shuffle (♪♪ played as ♪³♪)
Vocal 2nd time only

Words and Music by CHRISTOPHER WARD
and DAVID TYSON

Mis - sis - sip - pi in the mid - dle of a dry___ spell.
Up in Mem - phis the mu - sic's___ like a heat wave.

BLAZE OF GLORY
(From the Film "Young Guns II")

Words and Music by
JON BON JOVI

wake up   in   the morn - ing and I   raise my wear-y head,____   I've got an
night   I go to bed,   I pray the Lord my   soul   to keep._   No   I ain't

gun.

Additional Lyrics (Album version)

2. When you're brought into this world
    They say you're born in sin.
    Well, at least they gave me something
    I didn't have to steal or have to win.
    Well, they tell me that I'm wanted
    Yeah, I'm a wanted man.
    I'm a colt in your stable,
    I'm what Cain was to Abel.
    Mister, catch me if you can.

(Can't Live Without Your)
LOVE AND AFFECTION

Words and Music by MARC TANNER
MATT NELSON and GUNNAR NELSON

love.

With your love, _____ I put my arms a - round__ you.

DON'T LET THE SUN GO DOWN ON ME

Words and Music by ELTON JOHN
and BERNIE TAUPIN

I can't find oh ___ the right ro -

man -tic line. ____ But see me once _

and see the way _ I feel. ____

Don't dis - card me just be - cause_ you think _

GONNA MAKE YOU SWEAT
(EVERYBODY DANCE NOW)

Words and Music by ROBERT CLIVILLES
and FREDERICK B. WILLIAMS

Moderately Bright Rap

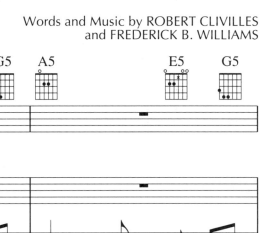

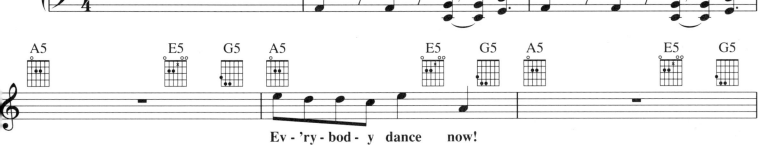

Ev - 'ry - bod - y dance now!

Ev - 'ry - bod - y dance now!

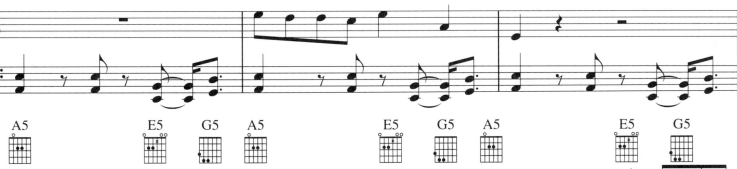

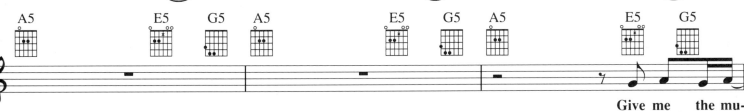

Give me the mu-

- sic.

Give me the mu - sic.

OPPOSITES ATTRACT

Words and Music by
OLIVER LEIBER

Moderate Funk Rock

1. Ba - by, seems we nev - er
2. Our friends are say - in'
3. Who'd a thought we
4-5. *See additional lyrics*

ev - er a - gree.___ You like the mov - ies, and I like T.___ V.
ain't gon - na last,___ 'cause I move slow - ly, and ba - by I'm_ fast.
we could be lov - ers? She makes the bed and he steals the cov - ers.

Additional Lyrics

4. She's got the money, and he's always broke.
   I don't like cigarettes, and I like to smoke.
   Things in common, just ain't a one.
   But when we get together we have nothin' but fun.

5. Baby, ain't it somethin' how we lasted this long?
   You and me provin' everyone wrong.
   Don't think we'll ever get our differences patched.
   Don't really matter 'cause we're perfectly matched.

HOW AM I SUPPOSED TO LIVE WITHOUT YOU

Words and Music by MICHAEL BOLTON
and DOUG JAMES

swept your heart _ a - way____ from the look up - on _ your face _ I see it's true.__
built my world _ a-round____ the hope that one _ day we'd be so much more than

____ friends?____

So tell me all a-bout it, tell me 'bout the plans you're mak-
I don't want to know the price_ I'm gon-na pay for dream-

- in', _____ oh__ tell me one thing more____ be - fore_ I go._
- in', _____ oh__ e-ven now it's more_ than I can take._

_____ } Tell me how am I ___ sup-posed ___ to live _ with-out _

I DON'T HAVE THE HEART

Words and Music by ALLAN RIC
and JUD FRIEDMA

RELEASE ME

Words and Music by CARNIE WILSON
WENDY WILSON and CHYNNA PHILLIPS

SET ADRIFT ON MEMORY BLISS

Words and Music by ATTRELL CORDES
and GARY KEMP

MCA music publishing

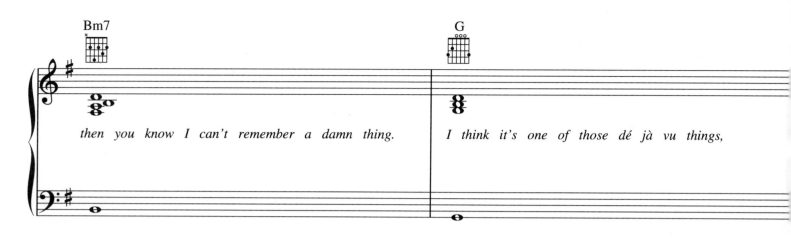

then you know I can't remember a damn thing.   I think it's one of those dé jà vu things,

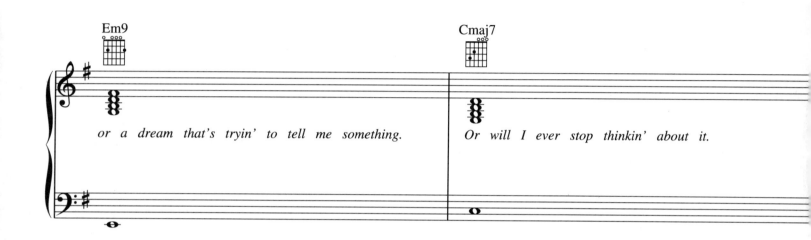

or a dream that's tryin' to tell me something.   Or will I ever stop thinkin' about it.

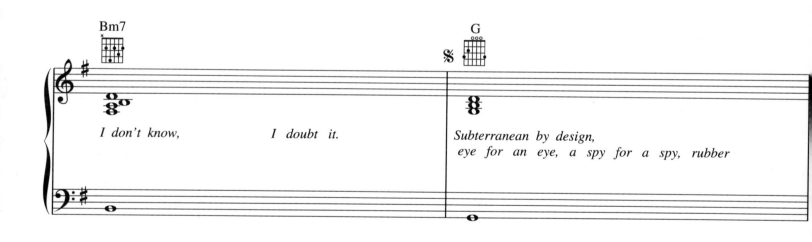

I don't know,   I doubt it.   Subterranean by design,
eye for an eye, a spy for a spy, rubber

I wonder what I would find   if I | met you, let my eyes caress you, until | I meet the thought of Misses Princess Who?
bands expand   in a frustrating sigh.   Tell | me that she's not dreaming. She's got | an ace in the hole, it doesn't have meaning.

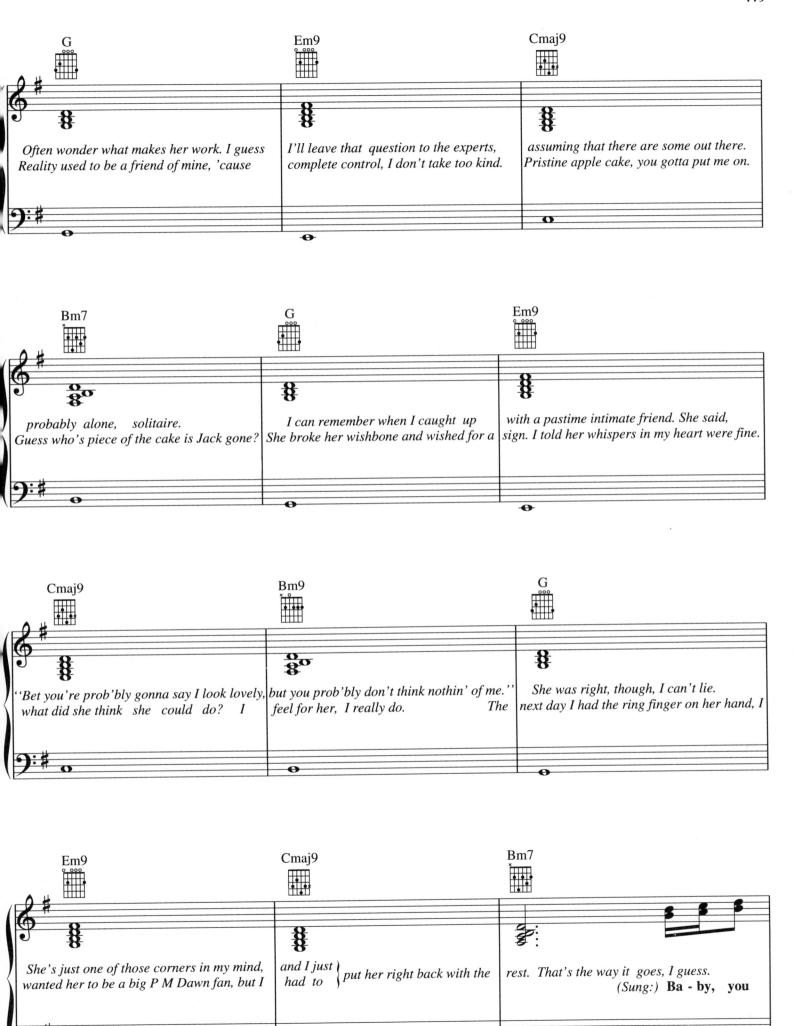

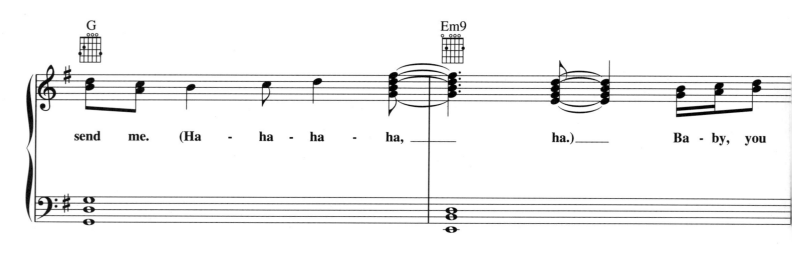

send me. (Ha - ha - ha - ha, _____ ha.) _____ Ba - by, you

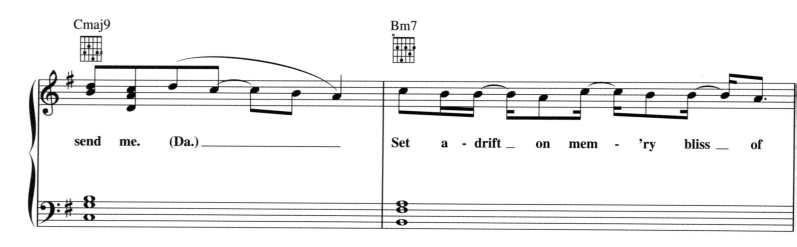

send me. (Da.) _____ Set a - drift _ on mem - 'ry bliss _ of

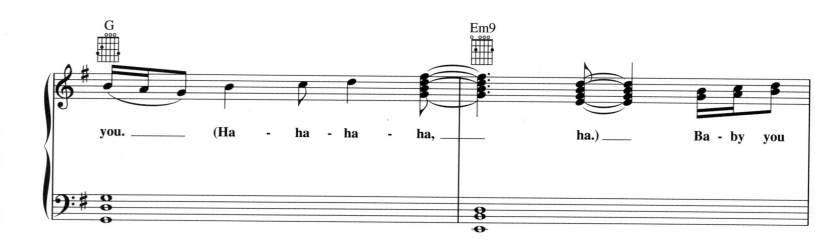

you. _____ (Ha - ha - ha - ha, _____ ha.) ___ Ba - by you

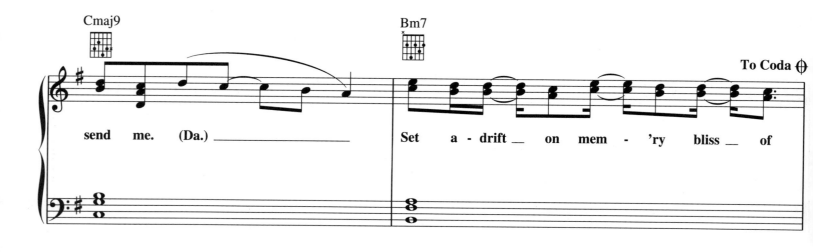

To Coda ⊕

send me. (Da.) _____ Set a - drift __ on mem - 'ry bliss __ of

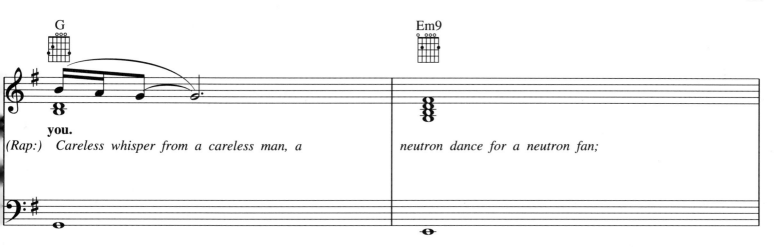

G

you.
(Rap:) Careless whisper from a careless man, a

Em9

neutron dance for a neutron fan;

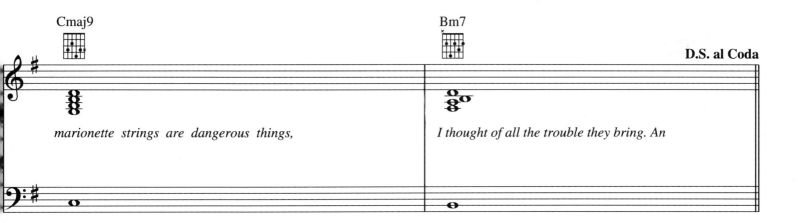

Cmaj9

marionette strings are dangerous things,

Bm7

D.S. al Coda

I thought of all the trouble they bring. An

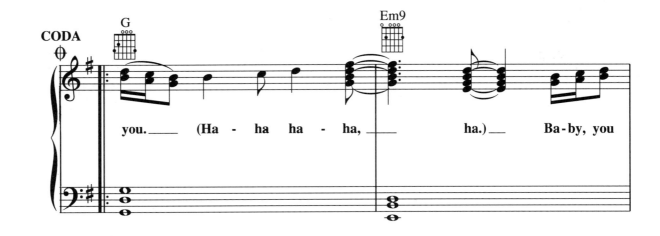

CODA

G

you.___ (Ha - ha ha - ha,___ ha.)___ Ba - by, you

Em9

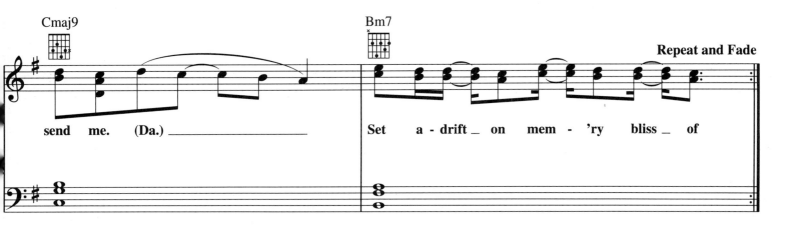

Cmaj9

Repeat and Fade

send me. (Da.) _____

Bm7

Set a - drift_ on mem - 'ry bliss_ of

SAVE THE BEST FOR LAST

Words and Music by PHIL GALDSTO
JON LIND and WENDY WALDMA

STEP BY STEP

Words and Music by
MAURICE STARR

TO BE WITH YOU

By ERIC MARTIN
and DAVID GRAHAM

it's through, _ it's through. _ And fate will twist _ the both _ of you. _____ So

come on, ba - by, come on o - ver. Let me be _ the one _ to show _ you.

When

YOU'RE IN LOVE

Words and Music by GLEN BALLARD, CARNIE WILSON,
WENDY WILSON and CHYNNA PHILLIPS

O-pen the door___ and come in. ___

I'm___ so glad to see you my friend. ___

I

MCA music publishing

Repeat and Fade

VISION OF LOVE

Words and Music by MARIAH CAREY
and BEN MARGULIES